Streets in VICTORIAN TIMES

Margaret Stephen

WAYLAND

Victorian Times

Christmas in Victorian Times

Clothes in Victorian Times

Schools in Victorian Times

Streets in Victorian Times

Sundays in Victorian Times

Transport in Victorian Times

How we Learn About the Victorians

Queen Victoria reigned from 1837 to 1901, a time when Britain went through enormous social and industrial changes. We can learn about Victorians in various ways. Many buildings built in Victorian times can still be seen today. We can also look at their documents, maps and artefacts – many of which can be found in museums. Photography, invented during Victoria's reign, gives us a good picture of life in Victorian Britain. In this book you will see what Victorian life was like through some of this historical evidence.

Editor: Carron Brown
Designer: Joyce Chester
Cosultant: Norah Granger

First published in 1996 by Wayland Publishers Ltd,
61 Western Road, Hove, East Sussex BN3 1JD, England

© Copyright 1996 Wayland Publishers Ltd

British Library Cataloguing in Publication Data
Stephen, Margaret
Streets in Victorian Times
    1. City and town life – Great Britain – History – 19th century – Juvenile literature
    2. Great Britain – Social conditions – 19th century – Juvenile literature
    I. Title
    941'.08
ISBN 0 7502 1877 0

Typeset by Joyce Chester
Printed and bound in Great Britain by B.P.C. Paulton Books

Text based on *Streets: Victorian Life* by Richard Wood published by Wayland Publishers Ltd in 1993.

Cover picture: A busy Victorian street in London.

Picture acknowledgements
E. T. Archive *cover*, 4, 12, 20, 21 (bottom), 23; Mary Evans 5 (top), 6 (Bruce Castle Museum), 7 (top), 8, 9, 10, 11 (left), 13 (top), 14, 15 (bottom), 16, 17, 18, 19 (bottom), 21 (top), 24, 26 (bottom), 27; Hulton Deutsch Picture Library 7 (bottom), 19 (top), 25 (bottom); Mansell Collection 25 (top); Sefton 13 (bottom); Salvation Army 26 (top); Tate Gallery, London 22; Richard Wood 5 (bottom), 11 (right). The artwork on page 15 is by Annabel Spenceley.

Contents

On the Street

A street can be a very busy place. People may live there, work there, go to the theatre or meet friends there, just as Victorian people did. But Victorian streets looked different from the streets we know today. The sounds and smells of the streets were also different in Victorian times.

A London Street

Can you spot differences between the street in the picture and a street today?

Look at:

- the chimneys for coal fires
- the rough road surface
- the street sellers
- the clothes people wore
- the shop-fronts

Do you see any traffic?

The Strand in London, in 1825. ▶

A Village Street

Streets in villages were very quiet. Neighbours and friends chatted at their garden gates. Poor people were not supposed to speak to richer people unless they were spoken to first.

Street Names

Towns quickly grew larger in Victorian times. Houses in new streets often all looked the same.
To help people find the new addresses, houses were given numbers and streets were given names. Iron name plates such as the one below were put up at the end of each street. Victoria Road was a new street name used in many towns during Queen Victoria's reign.

▲ The people in the photograph above are chatting about the news of the day, in 1875.

The name plate for Victoria Road. ▼

·VICTORIA·ROAD

Horse Buses

There were other changes as towns grew bigger. Many people had to travel further to go to work or to shop. Rich people owned horses and carriages. From 1829, there were horse-drawn buses called omnibuses. Many people travelled in them. An omnibus could fit 12 people inside and 10 people on the top. The driver had to sit on the outside, even in bad weather. Buses had advertisements on them for goods such as soap.

A London horse bus, in about 1900. ▼

Crossing Sweepers

Victorian streets were very dirty. People threw rubbish into open drains. The streets were very messy because there were so many horses. Road surfaces were cracked by the iron wheels of carts, carriages and buses. In summer, the roads were dusty and in winter, they were covered in mud. Rich people paid a crossing sweeper to brush a path for them to cross the road. It was difficult for ladies to keep their long dresses clean.

▲ This drawing shows a crossing sweeper in about 1900.

Motor Cars

In the 1890s, motor cars were quite new. Only rich people could afford to buy them. At first, a man holding a red flag had to walk in front of each car to warn people of the car's approach. From 1896, flags were no longer used and the speed limit went up from 16 kph to 23 kph. Cars made the streets noisier and busier.

▲ Victorian motor cars.

Street Services

Today, piped water, drains and electricity run through our streets. We can telephone for help from the police, the fire brigade or the ambulance service. The post is delivered to our houses. In Victorian times, most people did not have the services we have now.

Street Lighting

In the 1830s, many gas lamps were put up in town streets. The lamplighter went round lighting each lamp in the evening and turning them all off in the morning. Around 50 years later, large towns began to use electric lights. Bright lighting made the streets safer for people after dark.

This drawing shows a lamplighter in the 1840s. ▶

Water Pump

At home, we just turn on a tap if we need clean water. In Victorian times, people usually had to fetch water from a river, from wells or from a street pump. Carrying buckets of water was heavy work. People were careful not to spill it. They did not want to waste any water.

This woman is filling a jug with water from a village pump. ▶

The Spread of Disease

Many people were crowded together in houses, with no clean water and no proper drains, so diseases spread very quickly. People often died of diseases such as cholera and typhoid. Posters were put up to warn everyone of an outbreak of disease, and to offer free advice at any time of day or night.

This is a cholera warning poster from 1866. ▶

BOARD OF WORKS
FOR THE LIMEHOUSE DISTRICT.
COMPRISING LIMEHOUSE, RATCLIFF, SHADWELL & WAPPING.

In consequence of the appearance of CHOLERA within this District, the Board have appointed the under-mentioned Medical Gentlemen who will give ADVICE, MEDICINE, AND ASSISTANCE, FREE OF ANY CHARGE, AND UPON APPLICATION, AT ANY HOUR OF THE DAY OR NIGHT.

The Inhabitants are earnestly requested not to neglect the first symptoms of the appearance of Disease, (which in its early stage is easy to cure), but to apply, WITHOUT DELAY, to one of the Medical Gentlemen appointed.

The Board have opened an Establishment for the reception of Patients, in a building at Green Bank, near Wapping Church, (formerly used as Wapping Workhouse), where all cases of Cholera and Diarrhœa will be received and placed under the care of a competent Resident Medical Practitioner, and proper Attendants.

THE FOLLOWING ARE THE MEDICAL GENTLEMEN TO BE APPLIED TO;--

Mr. ORTON,
56, White Horse Street.

Dr. NIGHTINGALL,
4, Commercial Terrace, Commercial Road, (near Limehouse Church.)

Mr. SCHROEDER,
53, Three Colt Street, Limehouse.

Mr. HARRIS,
5, York Terrace, Commercial Road, (opposite Stepney Railway Station.)

Mr. CAMBELL,
At Mr. GRAY's, Chemist, Old Road, opposite " The World's End."

Mr. LYNCH,
St. James's Terrace, Back Road, Shadwell.

Mr. HECKFORD,
At the Dispensary, Wapping Workhouse.

BOARD OFFICES, WHITE HORSE STREET,
26th July, 1866.

By ORDER,
THOS. W. RATCLIFF,
Clerk to the Board.

Dirty Drains

In 1853, a doctor found that dirty water was to blame for illnesses such as cholera. At that time, the water in wells and rivers was polluted by the dirt from drains.

In London, in the 1860s, pipes were laid to houses so that people could have clean water. Sewers were built below the streets to take away the filthy waste from toilets and drains. People were then able to keep themselves cleaner and healthier than before.

▲ These men are climbing down to inspect the sewers underneath a street in 1890.

Fire Brigade

Victorians used open fires for heating and cooking. They used candles and oil or gas lamps for light. It is not surprising that Victorian houses often caught fire. Because houses were built so close together, fire spread quickly.

From the 1860s, fire engines were pulled by horses and carried a steam pump, hoses and a tank of water. In some towns, fires were sprayed with water from a pipe under the road.

◀ The Southampton fire brigade in 1885.

The Penny Post

In 1840, Rowland Hill started the Penny Post. Stamps showed Queen Victoria's head. At first, letters were posted at post offices. But, from 1852, pillar boxes were put in the streets. At first they were not red, but green in colour. Some Victorian pillar boxes are still used today.

▲ A Victorian pillar box in Norwich.

Buildings on the Street

There were different kinds of buildings on Victorian streets. Some were old buildings, but others were new. Many are still being used today. Perhaps your house or school was built in Victorian times. There may be a date on your school building to tell you how old it is.

The Busy High Street

By 1898, some busy streets had lampposts, telephone wires, large shop windows and advertisements. Many wealthy people had moved out of big towns to live in the suburbs, but town centres were still busy. Look again at the picture on page 4 to see how streets had changed in the years between 1825 and 1898.

Kensington High Street in London, in1898. ▼

Homes for Poor People

Poor families often had to share a small house. In big cities, such as London, Glasgow and Edinburgh, blocks of flats were built to give homes to many poorer families. People liked having their own new homes.

New housing for the poor in 1879. ▼

Public Buildings

Victorians built large, grand, public stone or plaster buildings, such as churches, stations and town halls. These buildings had a lot of decoration. Many important buildings had statues of famous people on them or in the street nearby. Coloured bricks and other building materials could be brought by train from other parts of the country.

Manchester Town Hall. ▲

Victorian Terraced Houses

New houses were often built in terraces. Many of these houses looked the same. They were cheap to build because they shared side walls. Some had tiny yards and some had no yards or gardens at all. There was sometimes a shop at the end of the row of houses. Some terraced houses had front and back gardens. They cost more to buy.

Houses such as the one in the drawing opposite cost £150 to build. They had a hall, a front parlour and three bedrooms. There was no bathroom but, at the back, there was a scullery and a flush toilet. Sometimes, the toilet was outside the house in the back yard. Many terraced houses were built in Victorian times, and some are still lived in today.

◄ This drawing shows how close together Victorian terraced houses were built.

Front

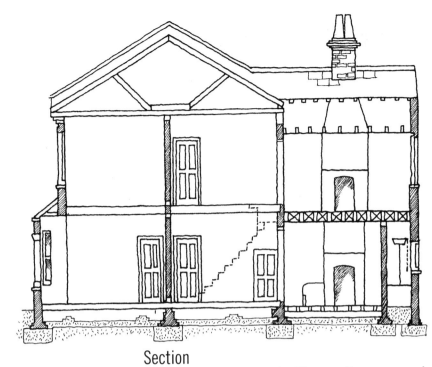

Section

▲ These diagrams show a terraced house from the front and side.

Street Furniture

Before Victorian times, buildings in Britain were made only from the building materials that could be found nearby. But from the 1850s, trains could take building materials to any part of Britain. The iron objects in the picture came from ironworks in the north of England. You will see from the picture that street furniture made of iron (such as lampposts) was very popular at that time.

▼ Cast-iron street fittings.

Homes in the Street

In big towns, richer people often lived in large, detached houses, in areas with wide streets lined with trees. Poorer factory workers lived in smaller houses in another part of the town. Their homes were usually on narrow streets with no trees.

Living in the Countryside

People often lived in the same village all their lives. They knew each other well and often married people from their own village.
Life was hard for poor country people. They lived in small, dark cottages and did not earn much money for the work they did. They did not have piped water in their homes or the services that many town people enjoyed. People had to carry water from the village pump. People sometimes moved to towns to look for better jobs.

A village street, in about 1875. ▼

A Town Family

The family in the picture below lived in a large house. Father (Papa) probably travelled by train or cab to his office. Mother (Mama) spent her time reading, sewing or visiting friends, while maids did the housework and the cooking. The children went to private schools. They did not mix with poorer children. In Victorian times, a family with four children was a small family.

▼ A wealthy family returning home in 1855.

Rich Suburbs

Wealthy families lived in suburbs on the edge of towns. Their houses were set back from the street and had gardens around them. These houses had large rooms, but maids slept in small rooms high up in the attic. Servants and tradespeople were not allowed to use the front door.

▲ This detached house was built in the 1890s.

Maid of All Work

Many families could afford to employ a maid to do all sorts of work for them. The maid cleaned, cooked, washed, mended clothes and nursed the children. She worked long hours, from 6 o'clock in the morning to 10 o'clock at night. She had only half a day off each week. Richer people had more servants, such as a cook and a nanny. Very rich people even had a butler.

◄ A maid cleaning steps, in the 1870s.

Poor Families

Life was very hard for poor families in Victorian times. A whole family often lived in just one room. The children shared a bed. They only had rags for bedclothes to keep them warm. When their parents had some work, they could buy bread and potatoes to eat. If there was no work, there was no food and the children went hungry. Children often worked to earn a little money to help their families.

A poor family in London's East End, in the 1900s. ▼

Narrow Alleyways

Between some houses there were dark alleys (called wynds in Scotland). Poor people lived in the houses behind. Their houses were small and damp, with no clean water or drains. The air was dirty with smoke from the chimneys. In the 1840s, over half of the poor children in towns such as Manchester died before they were five years old.

A narrow alleyway, or wynd in Edinburgh, in about 1840. ▲

Work in the Street

Many people today work in shops or markets in the street. In Victorian times, people also worked in places like these. It was difficult for some people to earn enough to feed and clothe their families.

The Butcher

Victorian shops were small. The butcher in the picture below probably lived above the shop. Today, butchers do not hang meat outside their shops. One reason is that meat could be covered in dirt from busy roads.

This photograph of a butcher's shop in Surrey was taken in about 1900. ▼

Groceries were sold loose. They were cut up and weighed for each customer. Sometimes, shopping was delivered to richer people in a cart like the one in the picture.

The Blacksmith

In early Victorian times, the village blacksmith made iron objects by hand. Later on, such goods were made in factories and sent by train all over Britain. But blacksmiths were still busy. They made shoes and harnesses for all the horses on the streets and on farms. Most places had a blacksmith's shop, called a 'smithy'.

▼ A blacksmith's shop.

A shoe black at work, in 1892. ▶

Working on the Street

The man in the picture on the right earned money on the street as a shoe black. Shoe blacks cleaned shoes.

Some people made goods in their homes. They made shirts, hats and lace cloths for shops and factories. Some children worked at home but, after 1880, all children under 10 years old had to go to school. They were not allowed to work all day.

The Market-Place

Streets were full of life on market days. Shoppers looked round the stalls for bargains.

Country people came with their carts of eggs and cheese, live hens and rabbits to sell. Fishermen sold oysters and mussels. Travelling salesmen sold books, china and glass. The market was noisy as sellers shouted to attract customers. On the street there were also cows, pigs and sheep being led to the livestock market.

Norwich market-place in the 1830s. ▼

Street Sellers

There were street sellers in large towns in Victorian times. Many were poorly dressed. Their second-hand clothes were patched and torn. Some people bought the street sellers' goods because they felt sorry for them. It was very hard to earn enough money to live.

▲ A match seller, in 1892.

Victorians often bought food on the street. In the picture on the right there is an oven on the cart. It was wheeled from street to street. Hot potatoes cost 1d (less than 1p) each. Poor people liked hot potatoes from the oven. Many poor people did not have an oven at home.

A baked potato seller, in 1892. ▲

Street Life

Victorian streets were often busy and noisy places all day long. There was entertainment on the street for children to enjoy. Children could play on the streets because there were no cars or buses.

Street Entertainment

Children liked to listen to the organ grinder's music on their way home from school. They watched as he turned the handle and the organ played tunes they knew well. The organ grinder's monkey danced to the music. Then it held out a hat to beg from people passing by. Today, in Britain, people are not allowed to use animals for entertainment on the street.

◀ An organ grinder, in 1886.

The Muffin Man

The muffin man rang his bell and called, 'muffins, fresh muffins'. People heard his cry and knew that he had brought fresh muffins for breakfast or tea.

Street sellers all had their own cries. Here are some of the cries: 'ropes of onions', 'rags and bones', 'buy a dish of eels', 'oranges fresh and fair', 'sweep, sweep, chimney sweep', 'knives to grind'. The knife grinder sent sparks flying as he sharpened knives.

◄ A muffin man, in about 1900.

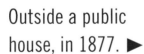
Outside a public house, in 1877. ►

Public Houses

Most main streets in towns had at least one public house. The customers were mostly men. They drank beer from large mugs. Sometimes, they played cards or had a game of skittles after work. In summer, they sat outside.

The Pie Shop

Meat or eel pies were sold for 1d or 2d (1p). This was a lot of money for children with no shoes and only ragged clothes. Sometimes, children begged for food and sometimes, they went hungry. Many people were very poor even at the end of Queen Victoria's long reign. But for some people life slowly became easier.

◄ Poor children outside a pie shop, in about 1900.

Street Crime

Because streets were not well lit, it was easy to steal and to pick pockets. Some people stole food for their families to eat. In 1829, Sir Robert Peel set up Britain's first paid police force. Policemen were called 'bobbies' or 'peelers' after Robert Peel. They wore blue coats and hats.

There was less crime after that on the streets. By 1901 there were thousands of policemen in Britain.

▲ London police arrest a thief, in 1869.

Street Parties

In 1897, Queen Victoria had been queen for 60 years. To celebrate, there were many parties in the streets all over Britain.

This is the queen's Diamond Jubilee procession, in 1897. ▼

Britain was then the richest country in the world. Streets were cleaner and safer than in 1837. Diseases did not kill so many people and most people had a better life than ever before.

Timeline

Early 1800s

1825
First railway is built by George Stephenson, from Stockton to Darlington.

1829
Sir Robert Peel's Police Act starts a police force in London.

Horse-drawn bus service begins.

1830s

1831
Population of Britain is 16 million people.

1833
Children under 18 forbidden to work more than 12 hours a day.

1834
Serious outbreak of cholera.

1837
Victoria becomes queen.

1839
First bicycle is invented.

Photography is invented.

1840s

1840
Children forbidden to sweep chimneys.

1845
Official reports on the living conditions of poor people.

1848
Electric lights first shown in London.

Serious outbreak of cholera.

1850s

1851
Many new inventions on show at The Great Exhibition at Crystal Palace, London.

1852
Pillar boxes first placed on streets.

1853
Discovery that cholera is carried in polluted drinking water.

1856
All counties ordered to set up police forces.

1860s

1865
First proper sewage system built in London.

1867
Dr Barnardo opens his first home for homeless orphans.

1870s

1870
Rubber tyres first used.

Telephone invented by Alexander Graham Bell.

1874
Factory Act forbids children to work more than 10 hours a day.

1875
Clearance of slum houses to build new homes for the poor.

1879
First London streets lit by electricity.

1880s

1880
School is compulsory for all children up to the age of 10.

Penny farthing bicycle is invented.

1885
First motor car is invented.

1889
Inflated rubber tyres invented.

1890s

1896
Motor cars are allowed to travel up to 22 kph without a red flag.

1897
Queen Victoria's 60 years as queen celebrated.

1900s

1901
Population of Britain now 37 million people.

Coal tar first used to make smooth road surfaces.

Death of Queen Victoria.

Glossary

Alleyway A narrow passage between buildings.

Attic A room at the top of a house, under the roof.

Blacksmith Someone who makes objects out of iron.

Butler The head servant in a house.

Cholera A dangerous disease caused by drinking dirty water.

Detached houses Houses that stand on their own.

Diamond Jubilee A special anniversary to celebrate 60 years.

Grind To sharpen on a stone.

Harnesses Leather straps to put on horses to pull carts.

Livestock Farm animals.

Nanny A maid who looks after children.

Omnibuses A Victorian word for buses.

Organ grinder A person who plays an organ on the street for money.

Parlour A room used for special occasions.

Scullery A room used for cleaning and washing.

Sewage Filthy waste from toilets and drains.

Sewers Underground pipes or tunnels for removing waste.

Skittles A game where a wooden ball is thrown at several standing wooden objects (called pins) to make them fall down. The person who makes the most fall down wins the game.

Slums Poor houses that are not fit for people to live in.

Suburbs Districts on the edges of towns or cities.

Terraces Rows of houses all joined together.

Typhoid A dangerous disease causing red spots on the skin.

Wynd A Scottish word for a narrow lane or alley.

Books to Read

Hicks, Peter, *The Victorians*
　(Wayland, 1995)
Parsons, Martin, *A Victorian Village*
　(Wayland, 1995)
Tanner, Q., *Rubbish*
　(A & C Black, 1991)
Triggs, Tony D., *Victorian Britain*
　(Wayland, 1989)

Places to Visit

The following museums have
displays and exhibitions about
Victorian times.

England
Berkshire: Museum of English Rural Life,
　Reading, RG6 2AG. Tel: 01734 318660
Birmingham: Museum of Science and Industry,
　Newhall Street, Birmingham, B3 1RZ.
　Tel: 0121 2353890
Cambridgeshire: City Museum and Art Gallery,
　Priestgate, Peterborough, PE1 1LF.
　Tel: 01733 343329
Cleveland: Preston Hall Museum, Yarm Road,
　Stockton-on-Tees, TS18 3RH.
　Tel: 01642 781184
County Durham: The North of England Open Air
　Museum, Beamish, County Durham,
　DH9 0RG. Tel: 01207 231811
Dorset: Waterfront Museum, Oakley's Mill,
　Paradise Street, The Quay, Poole, BH15 1HJ.
　Tel: 01202 683138
Lincolnshire: Museum of Lincolnshire Life, The
　Old Barracks, Burton Road, Lincoln, LN1 3LY.
　Tel: 01522 528448
London: London Transport Museum,
　Covent Garden, London, WC2E 7BB.
　Tel: 0171 3796344
　Museum of London, London Wall, London,

EC2Y 5HN. Tel: 0171 6003699
Manchester: Museum of Science and Industry,
　Liverpool Road Station, Castlefield,
　Manchester, M3 4JP. Tel: 0161 832 2244
Norfolk: Bridewell Museum of Trades and
　Industries, Bridewell Alley, Norwich,
　NR2 1AQ. Tel: 01603 667228
Nottinghamshire: Industrial Museum, Courtyard
　Buildings, Wollaton Park, Nottingham,
　NG8 2AE. Tel: 01602 284 602
Shropshire: Ironbridge Gorge Museum, Blists
　Hill Site, Telford, TS8 7AW. Tel: 01952 433522
West Midlands: The Black Country Museum,
　Tipton Road, Dudley, DY1 4SQ.
　Tel: 0121 5579643
Yorkshire and Humberside: Hull Museum of
　Transport, High Street, Hull, HU1 3DX.
　Tel: 01482 222737
　York Castle Museum, York, YO1 1RY.
　Tel: 01532 797326

Scotland
Lothian: Huntly House Museum,
　142 Canongate, Edinburgh, EH8 8DD.
　Tel: 0131 2252424 ext 6689
　National Museums of Scotland,
　Chamber Street, Edinburgh, EH1 1JF.
　Tel. 0131 2257534
Strathclyde: Museum of Transport, Kelvin Hall,
　1 Bunhouse Road, Glasgow, G3 8PZ.
　Tel: 0141 2219600
　Tenement House, 145 Buccleugh Street,
　Glasgow, G3 6QN. Tel: 0141 3330183

Wales
Cardiff: Welsh Folk Museum, St. Fagans, Cardiff,
　CF5 6XB. Tel: 01222 569441
　Welsh Industrial and Maritime Museum, Bute
　Street, Cardiff, CF1 6AN. Tel: 01222 485321
Swansea: Swansea Maritime and Industrial
　Museum, Museum Square, Maritime Quarter,
　Swansea, SA1 1SN. Tel: 01792 650351

Northern Ireland
Belfast: Ulster Folk and Transport Museum,
　Witham Street Gallery, Belfast, BT4 1HP.
　Tel: 01232 428428

Index